Kertu Sillaste

I AM AN ARTIST

This book belongs to:

_____

_____

_____

Kertu Sillaste

GRAFFEG

SELF-PORTRAIT

SELF-PORTRAIT

An artist thinks and draws and paints and glues and sketches and moulds and photographs and films and considers and constructs and assembles.

I think that the most important thing when making art, is a GOOD IDEA.

A good idea comes when you take out paper and paints.

A good idea comes when you start imagining things.

There are all kinds of thoughts.

"I'll only take pictures of shadows."

"I'll draw a world where nothing is like it is in the real world."

"I'll put clothes on chairs."

"I'll paint a new view on a window."

"I'll draw everything bad in the world and then erase it."

I'll gather dust curls in a box and make a big, soft, grey statue out of them.

I'll build as tall a tower as I can from all my things.

I'll make a green video.

I'll wrap everything in foil.

I'll trample a long winding trail in grass.

Some ideas are so good, I'll start working on them immediately.

One time I discovered that
art is a game.

MEMORIAL FOR GRANDMA

MEMORIAL FOR GRANDPA

I'll take a piece from here, a piece from there, combine them in my own way and...
Wham! Ready!

AUNT ANNIE

POOR RULER

And another time I thought that

art is a puzzle.

What could be in this picture?

But yesterday I felt that
art is finding

CLEANER

STORK

TERRIFYING BOAT RIDE

HUNTER MOOSE

Sometimes, I think that

art is telling stories through pictures.

Some pictures are of what worries the artist.
Some pictures show what
makes the artist happy.

It's especially cool when
art is a surprise.

Ta-dah!
You've definitely never seen anything like this before!

An artist has lots of ideas.

I'll build new trees on stumps in the forest.

I'll invent a new plasticine and shape that old horseriding statue into something fun and colourful.

All ideas can't be made real.
And what of it?!
It's still fun to think.

Making art isn't always easy. Yesterday I drew almost a hundred tigers...

...and still wasn't quite satisfied.

But the next morning…

I'll be brave and show my work to others, even to my big brother. I'll worry a little about whether he will understand what I made, or laugh.

I'll be glad if he likes it.
An artist really needs praise.

This is me, John.
Here I am thinking that it's so great to be an artist because there is all kinds of art and you can make art in many different ways.

I am an Artist
Published in Great Britain in 2021 by Graffeg Limited.

Written, drawn and designed by Kertu Sillaste
copyright © 2021. Designed and produced by
Graffeg Limited copyright © 2021.

Originally published as *Mina Olen Kunstnik* in Estonia in 2018 by Koolibri.

English Translation of the Work © 2021 Adam Cullen.

Graffeg Limited, 24 Stradey Park Business Centre, Mwrwg Road, Llangennech, Llanelli, Carmarthenshire, SA14 8YP, Wales, UK.
Tel: 01554 824000. www.graffeg.com.

Kertu Sillaste is hereby identified as the author of this work in accordance with section 77 of the Copyrights, Designs and Patents Act 1988.

A CIP Catalogue record for this book is available from the British Library.

All rights reserved. No part of this publication may be reproduced, stored in a retrieval system or transmitted, in any form or by any means, electronic, mechanical, photocopying, recording or otherwise, without the prior permission of the publishers.

The publication of the book has been supported by the Cultural Endowment of Estonia and the Books Council of Wales.

ISBN 9781914079634

1 2 3 4 5 6 7 8 9